INTERFACT ™

THE BOOK AND CD THAT WORK TOGETHER

OCEANS

TWO CAN ™

LONDON ■ PRINCETON

www.two-canpublishing.com

**Published by Two-Can Publishing,
43–45 Dorset Street, London W1U 7NA**

© Two-Can Publishing 2001, 1997

For information on Two-Can books and multimedia,
call (0)20 7224 2440, fax (0)20 7224 7005, or visit our
website at http://www.two-canpublishing.com

Created by
act-two
346 Old Street
London EC1V 9RB

ISBN 1-85434-920-1

2 4 6 8 10 9 7 5 3 1

A catalogue record for this book is available from the British Library

Photograph credits: Image Bank/Kaz Mori: front cover; Ardea/Clem Haagner: p.6–7;
Greenpeace/Morgan: p.8; Ardea/François Gohier: p.9; Ardea/Ron & Valerie Taylor: p.11;
ZEFA/Dr D James: p.12–13; Planet Earth/Robert Arnold: p.14; Oxford Scientific Films/Peter Parks: p.15 (top & bottom);
Ardea/J-M Labat p.16 (top;) Oxford Scientific Films/GI Bernard: p.16 (bottom); Planet Earth/Peter David: p.17 (top left);
Planet Earth/Gillian Lythgoe: p17 (top right); Planet Earth/Peter Scoones: p.17 (bottom); Ardea/Ron & Valerie Taylor: p.18;
Planet Earth/Peter David: p.19; Ardea/Clem Haagner: p.20; Planet Earth: Ardea/Jim Brandenberg: p.21 (top);
Ardea/François Gohier: p.21 (bottom); B&C Alexander: p.22–23; Ardea/Richard Vaughan: p.24; ZEFA: p.25;
Ardea/François Gohier: p.26–27. Illustrations by Francis Mosley

Every effort has been made to acknowledge correctly and contact the source of
each picture and Two-Can Publishing apologises for any unintentional errors or
omissions which will be corrected in future editions of this book.

Printed in Hong Kong by Wing King Tong

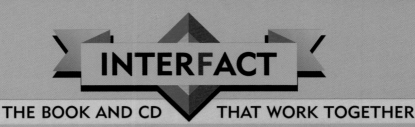

INTERFACT

THE BOOK AND CD ▽ THAT WORK TOGETHER

INTERFACT will have you hooked in minutes –
and that's a fact!

The disk is full of interactive
activities, puzzles, quizzes and games
that are fun to do
and packed with
interesting facts.

Get some frank answers
to all those vital questions
about oceans from
Frank Fish!

Open the
book and discover
more fascinating
information,
highlighted with
lots of full-colour
illustrations and
photographs.

Click on
Bubbles
for a
question

What lives below
the waves? Read
up and find out.

To get the most out of **INTERFACT**
use the book and disk together.
Look out for the special signs,
called Disk Links and Bookmarks.
To find out more, turn to page 43.

23

BOOKMARK

DISK LINK
Remember
how often
tides rise and
fall in order
to survive Shark Attack!

Once you've clicked on to
INTERFACT you'll never
look back.

LOAD UP!
Go to **page 40** to find out how to load
your disks and click into action.

What's on the disk

HELP SCREEN

Learn how to use the disk in no time at all.

Welcome to the
INTERFACT
disk on Oceans

To have a look at all the different things on the disk, simply click the <u>arrow keys</u> with your mouse.

As you do this, you'll see a description of each activity in the <u>reading box</u>.

Click on the picture at the top of the screen to select the activity you want to investigate.

These are the controls the Help Screen will tell you how to use:

- arrow keys
- reading boxes
- 'hot' words

FRANK FISH

If you've got a question, Frank has got the answer!

Why is the sea salty?

Get ready to go fishing for facts with Bubbles the sea horse! You'll receive frank answers to all your questions about seas, oceans, tides and waves from Frank Fish.

DEPTH GAUGE

Fathom out what goes on at different depths of the ocean!

The ocean floor is very cold. Here the temperature is between 1°C and 4°C.

Explore an interactive cross section of the ocean. Learn about the different zones in the sea and the amazing animals that live in them.

CREATURE FEATURE

Go animal crackers and learn more about sea life.

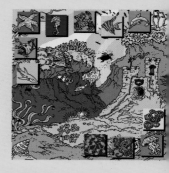

Help a tiny fish find its way home by working out the identity of mystery sea creatures and answering true or false questions.

OCEAN EXPLORER

Investigate all of the world's major oceans, seas, gulfs and bays.

Set off on a marine voyage of discovery aboard the fabulous Ocean Explorer! Find out all you need to know about the world's most important seas, oceans, gulfs and bays.

SOMETHING FISHY IS GOING ON

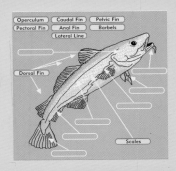

Learn about the different parts of a fish's body.

When it comes to a fish's anatomy, do you know a pectoral fin from a pelvic fin? Try putting the correct labels on the interactive picture of a cod and find out!

MAKE YOUR OWN CORAL REEF

Get creative and conjure up a coral reef!

Build your very own coral reef on screen. Once your picture is finished, you can print it out to colour in and keep.

SHARK ATTACK

Get your teeth into the quiz or the sharks will get their teeth into you!

Put your knowledge to the test, as you try to escape from the hungry sharks. All the answers are found in the book and on the disk.

What's in the book

Looking at the oceans

More than two-thirds of the world's surface is covered by vast oceans. They are the oldest and largest living **environments** and life began here more than 3,500 million years ago. But, although oceans dominate the world map, we have only just begun to explore their hidden depths.

Without the water in the oceans, the Earth would be dry, barren and devoid of life. Beneath its surface lie rugged mountains, active volcanoes, vast plateaux and seemingly bottomless **trenches**. The deepest ocean trenches could easily swallow up the tallest mountains on land!

Seen from above, the world's oceans appear empty and unchanging, but beneath the surface hides a unique world where water takes the place of air. A fantastic and rich mix of plants and animals live in these waters, from minute **plankton** to the giant blue whale.

DID YOU KNOW?

● Salt is not the only substance found in sea water. There are also tiny traces of gold, silver, uranium and other valuable **minerals.**

● Sound travels through water five times faster than through air. Dolphins navigate through the oceans by bouncing sounds off their surroundings and listening to their **echo.**

● Humans reached the deepest spot in the ocean for the first time in 1960.

DISK LINK
Dive into the ocean and explore the amazing world under the waves for yourself in DEPTH GAUGE.

▶ Animals can travel freely through the water. Most sea animals breathe underwater, but some, such as dolphins and whales, need to come up to the surface for air.

◀ In the Tropics, the oceans are warm and clear. But around the North and South **Poles** it is very cold and parts of the ocean are always frozen. Huge chunks of ice, called icebergs, float here.

Dividing the seas

Strictly speaking, there is really only one ocean. It stretches from the North **Pole** to the South Pole and encircles the globe. However, because **continents** divide the water, four separate oceans are recognised – the Pacific, the Atlantic, the Indian and the Arctic. Within these oceans are smaller bodies of water called seas, **bays** and **gulfs** that are cut off from the open oceans by land formations.

The Pacific is the largest and deepest of the four great oceans. It covers more of the world's surface than all of the continents put together. The word Pacific means peaceful but the water can be very rough. Waves of 34m tall have been recorded in the Pacific Ocean.

The Atlantic is the second biggest ocean, covering one-fifth of the world's surface. It is also the most important ocean for business – and therefore the busiest. Boats regularly cross the Atlantic, carrying cargo between the Americas, Africa and Europe.

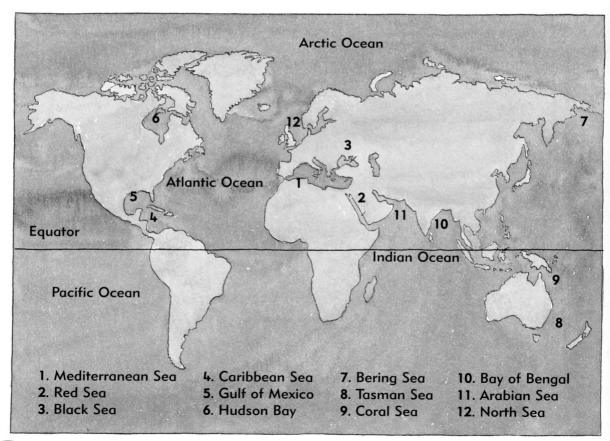

1. Mediterranean Sea
2. Red Sea
3. Black Sea
4. Caribbean Sea
5. Gulf of Mexico
6. Hudson Bay
7. Bering Sea
8. Tasman Sea
9. Coral Sea
10. Bay of Bengal
11. Arabian Sea
12. North Sea

DID YOU KNOW?

● It may take one drop of sea water 5,000 years to travel through all the world's oceans.

● The Atlantic Ocean is growing while the Pacific is shrinking. The continents move a few centimetres each year, so the relative sizes of the oceans are always changing.

● Greek divers are known to have reached depths of 22–30.5m in search of treasures. When a diver ran short of breath, he'd poke his head into a weighted diving bell, filled with air.

DISK LINK
Investigate the oceans and all the major seas, gulfs and bays using the OCEAN EXPLORER.

▲ In warm, tropical seas where the water is shallow and clear, there are vast, rocky structures known as **coral reefs**. These are made by small sea animals called polyps. Coral reefs support a greater variety of life than any other part of the oceans.

Moving waves

The world's oceans are always on the move. They travel in well-defined circular patterns called ocean **currents**. The currents flow like rivers, carrying warm water from the tropics and cold water from the **Poles**. Where two currents meet, the colder water sinks, pushing warmer water up to the surface.

There is also the regular movement of **tides**. Twice a day, all over the world, oceans rise and fall along the **coastlines**. These tides are linked to the pull on the Earth by the Moon and the Sun.

Tides and currents carry food and stir up the water, producing bubbles of oxygen which the sea animals need to breathe.

In the northern hemisphere, currents travel in a clockwise direction and in the southern hemisphere, they travel anti-clockwise.

DISK LINK
If you want to learn more about what causes the tides just ask FRANK FISH.

OCEAN POWER

● Giant whirlpools or maelstroms can occur where two fast-rushing currents are forced through narrow channels.

● Earthquakes and volcanoes on the sea bed can cause huge waves to crash on to the shore. These giant waves are known as tidal waves or **tsunamis.**

Food for life

Plants provide the basic food for life in the ocean, just as they do for life on land. Underwater plants are called **algae** and there are two main groups in the oceans.

The best known ocean algae are the seaweeds found around our coastlines. Limpets, periwinkles and other shoreline creatures graze on seaweeds, but these are not available to the animals of the open ocean.

The most important **marine** algae are called phytoplankton. These tiny, floating plants grow wherever sunlight penetrates the water. Huge clouds of phytoplankton drift in the upper layers of the ocean but they are too small to be seen with the naked eye.

Floating alongside and feeding upon the phytoplankton are tiny animals called zooplankton. This rich mix of plant and animal life, called **plankton**, is the foundation of all marine life.

PLANKTON FACTS

● Sailors crossing the ocean at night often see a soft glow on the water's surface. This is because some plankton produce flashes of blue-green light when they are disturbed.

● The very first life forms probably looked like today's phytoplankton.

● The largest animals in the world feed on plankton. Blue whales can weigh more than 90 tonnes and measure more than 30m in length. They sieve tiny shrimps called krill from the ocean, through a curtain of whalebone inside their mouths.

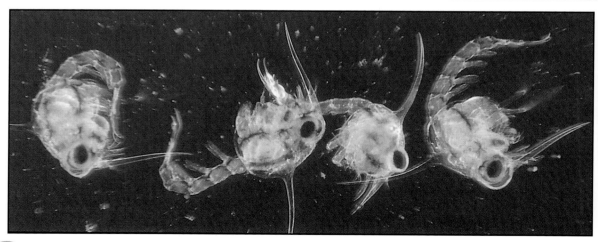

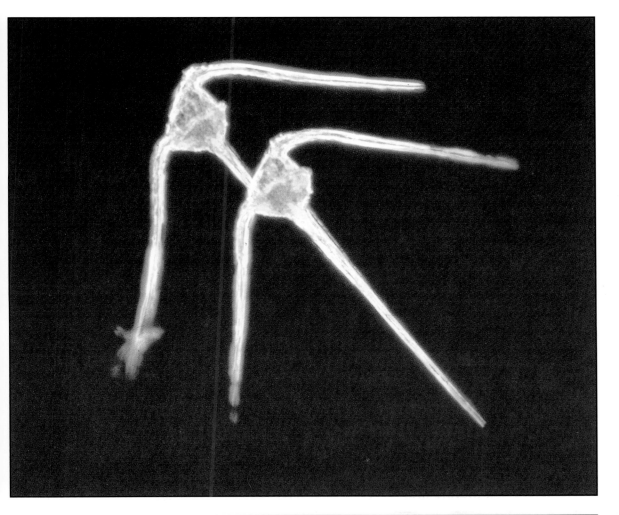

▲ ▶ Many of the tiny
floating plants that form
the phytoplankton join up
to make chains and
bracelets. Others float
alone and look like small
ice picks, ribbons or shells.

◀ Some zooplankton are
single-celled lifeforms.
Others are the larvae of
fish or other sea animals.

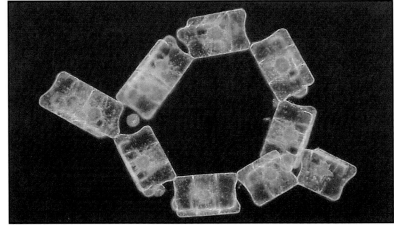

All shapes and sizes

There is a staggering variety of animals living in the world's oceans. Their size, shape and colour varies enormously from creature to creature. To some extent, each **marine** animal's appearance depends on its lifestyle and the ocean **environment** in which it lives. Sea anemones and sponges, for instance, stay rooted to the ocean floor for their entire lives and look more like plants than animals.

Fish are the most familiar marine creatures, but even their looks can be deceptive. Some species, such as eels, look more like snakes than fish. Others, such as the delicate sea horse, seem like a different kind of animal altogether.

▲ Many sea animals are a silvery-blue colour but some have bright, bold markings. The most colourful animals live in clear tropical waters. Their striking appearance helps them to establish territory and frighten off enemies.

◄ The octopus is one of many curious sea animals. It has eight arms, a short, rounded body and lives on the ocean bed. To swim, octopuses squirt water from a special siphon in their bodies.

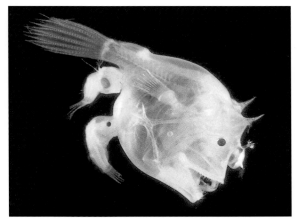

▲ The waters near the bottom of the oceans are cold and dark. Many deep-sea creatures have a light on their body that attracts prey. The deep-sea angler fish are very strange. If a male meets his mate, he attaches himself to her. After a time, his body breaks down into a sperm bag, which then fertilises the female's eggs.

▲ There are over 3,500 species of marine sponge living on the sea floor. Some form fleshy sheets, others, upright chimney stacks.

▶ The blue-spotted stingray is closely related to the shark. It floats over the surface of the sea bed, feeding on slugs and worms.

DISK LINK
Design your own beautiful underwater world in MAKE YOUR OWN CORAL REEF.

Hunters and the hunted

A great number of **marine** animals spend their entire lives sifting the water for **plankton** to feed on. However, they, in turn, are being hunted by other animals. It is estimated that for every ten animals that eat plankton, there is at least one hunter lurking nearby.

The shark is one of the most notorious and dangerous marine hunters. It is a perfectly-designed killing machine. The shark's body is streamlined for a fast life of hunting and its mouth is lined with razor-sharp teeth.

Although they have a reputation as man-eaters, only 25 of the 200 varieties of shark are actually dangerous to people. Sharks spend most of their time racing through the water in pursuit of their prey of fish, seals, turtles, small whales, other sharks and even sea birds.

Not all marine hunters are as fearsome as sharks. The pretty sea anemones look harmless, but they trap animals in their feathery tentacles. They then inject poison into their victim's body in a similar way to jellyfish.

DEFENCE FACTS

● Octopuses and cuttlefish squirt ink into the face of their attacker, giving themselves time to get away.

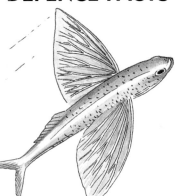

● Many sea animals, such as clams, live in shells. These act as armour, protecting the animal's soft body.

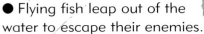

● Flying fish leap out of the water to escape their enemies.

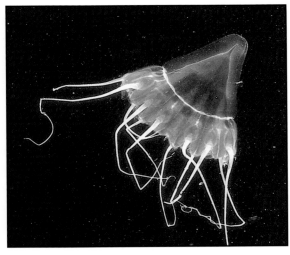

▲ Jellyfish, like sea anemones, catch prey in their trailing tentacles and poison them. Some of the most powerful poisons in the natural world are produced by jellyfish!

◄ Even when they are not chasing their next meal, sharks must keep moving all the time, otherwise they begin to sink.

Taking to the water

During the long passage of time, a small procession of land animals has returned to the oceans for their livelihood. Reptiles, mammals and even birds have braved the deep, salty waters to take advantage of the rich bounty of sea life.

Seals, turtles and penguins are some of the animals that have left dry land to colonise the oceans. Although they may spend most of their time in the sea, these creatures cannot breathe underwater like true sea animals, so they regularly visit the water's surface for air.

Whales are the most successful ocean colonisers. People often mistake them for fish, but they are, in fact, mammals. Whales spend their lives in the water, but most animals that have taken to the water must come back on land to **reproduce**.

DISK LINK
Test your knowledge of some more amazing creatures that live in the oceans in CREATURE FEATURE.

▲ Sea birds usually live on coastlines or on remote islands. But penguins spend more time than most sea birds actually swimming in the cold waters.

▲ Polar bears are marine mammals and spend most of their time hunting seals on or in the frozen Arctic Ocean. They are expert swimmers, and their wide, furry paws are webbed to help them swim more easily.

▶ Sea reptiles, such as turtles, are found in the warmer seas of the world. They lay their eggs on sandy beaches.

Ocean resources

People cannot live in the world's oceans but they have always harvested the rich waters. As the human population has increased, people have turned to the oceans more and more to increase their supply of food and raw materials. Today more than 70 billion kilograms of fish are caught each year and around one-fifth of the world's oil and gas is mined from the sea bed.

Modern fishing methods are often so intensive that they devastate fish communities and upset the balance of ocean life. Many of yesterday's most fertile seas are no longer able to support large fishing fleets because the fish stocks are so low.

The nets used by a large number of today's fishermen can also cause problems. They are made of nylon and do not rot underwater. If they are lost overboard, these nets become death traps to seals, dolphins and other **marine** creatures that cannot detect them.

DISK LINK
You can learn all about cod in SOMETHING FISHY IS GOING ON.

It is not only fish, such as cod and herring, that are in demand. Crabs and lobsters also prove to be popular seafood products. In addition, some whales and seals have been hunted to **extinction** for their meat, oil or fur.

▼ This North Sea trawler is small compared to the supertrawlers, which can be more than 90m long.

OCEAN PRODUCTS

● Fish oils are used to make glues, soaps and margarines.

● A rare gem called a **pearl** is formed inside the shells of certain oysters.

● Big nodules of iron, copper and **manganese** are lifted from the sea bed using suction pumps, or are raked into nets by dredging machines.

● In dry lands, seawater is sometimes treated to create a fresh water supply.

● Seaweed can be eaten like a vegetable and is also used to help make ice cream, toothpaste, paints and other everyday products.

Making the sea sick

Although we rely on the world's oceans for food, we treat them like rubbish bins. Waste is pumped and dumped into the water and **pesticides** and other man-made **pollutants** are washed into the ocean by rivers and streams.

The pollution of the world's oceans is harmful. Many sea animals are injured, strangled or suffocated each year because of floating debris called flotsam. The high level of **toxic** waste in a few seas is poisoning some animals and driving others away.

Land-locked seas, such as the Mediterranean, are among the most polluted waters.

▲ Oil spills threaten **marine** life. This poor sea bird will probably die unless the oil is cleaned from its feathers.

DISK LINK
Remember what you read in the book if you want to survive in SHARK ATTACK!

POLLUTION PROBLEMS

● Sealed barrels of dangerous radioactive and chemical waste have been dumped in some oceans, but no one knows if the containers are safe in the watery conditions.

● In some places around the world, pollution of the oceans has made local seafood unfit to eat.

▼ Busy ports can become deserted. The oil, sewage and litter spilled into the water makes a harbour unfit for sea life.

Save the oceans

Countries around the world are beginning to realise the importance of the oceans. International laws have been made to restrict the amount of waste put into the water and some **marine** mammals are now protected.

Countries on the shores of the dirtiest seas have begun clean-up programmes. But there is still a lot to be done.

In recent years, enormous damage has been caused in some oceans by oil tankers spilling their deadly cargo. Oil blocks out light from the oceans, upsetting **plankton** production and affecting all marine life. Through public pressure, oil companies could be persuaded to buy safer boats that would not leak in an accident.

Activities that were previously considered to be harmless have now been found to have damaging effects on marine life. The electric cables lying on the ocean floor disturb some seabed creatures and confuse many fish. Sharks bite into the cables, mistaking them for prey.

The noisy hustle and bustle from boats, busy coastal resorts and ocean-based industries frighten away seals, dolphins and other animals from their traditional breeding grounds.

Whales – the giants of the natural world – have been hunted for their oils and meat for so long that they are now difficult to find. As a result, they have become a strong international symbol of ocean conservation.

Most people agree that we must not kill any more whales and laws have now been made to protect the largest whale species. But, sadly, a few countries continue to hunt whales and eat their meat as an expensive delicacy.

Dakuwaca fights for his life

This tale is told by the people of Fiji, who depend on the ocean which surrounds them for food and transport.

Long ago, the sharks were the rulers of the islands that make up Fiji in the Pacific Ocean. Each island had its own particular shark who lived beside the reef entrance of the island. These sharks patrolled the waters of their territory, challenging anyone who dared to come near. They allowed friends in, but fought with hostile sharks until they paid a tribute.

Dakuwaca thought himself the greatest of all the sharks. He was big and fierce and enjoyed nothing better than a fight with another shark. He had never lost a fight and he was quite sure he never would. He cared nothing for the terrible storms which his fights caused, whipping up the waters so that the islanders were tossed about in their boats. Often island houses were swept away by massive waves from the ocean.

Dakuwaca was patrolling his reef one day when he came across a shark called Masilica. Masilica was the mischief maker among the sharks. He did not fight much himself but, with his wily ways, he had caused more fights than most sharks had fought!

"Good day, Dakuwaca," said Masilica. "I suppose you're off for another fight. It's amazing the way you always beat the other sharks. I wish I were as good a fighter as you."

"No other shark is as good a fighter as I am," said Dakuwaca. "Hardly anyone bothers to challenge me any more. They all know that I am so much stronger than them. In fact, it's getting very dull around here."

"Perhaps if you really want a good fight you should go over to Kandavu Island. I hear there's a creature well worth fighting there, a mighty monster which guards the reef so that it is impossible to go near it. But no-one ever goes there because they are much too afraid," said Masilica, with a sly glint in his eye. "Of course, I'm not suggesting that you're frightened, you're much too brave. And I'm sure none of the other sharks think that you're afraid either."

29

Dakuwaca thrashed his tail through the water. Of course he wasn't afraid, what a suggestion! But if the other sharks thought he was afraid, he had better do something at once. Almost before Masilica had finished speaking, Dakuwaca set off towards Kandavu, determined to challenge the fearsome monster.

As Dakuwaca approached Kandavu, he heard a deep, powerful voice calling from the shore. Dakuwaca had never heard anything like it before and he found himself trembling a little.

"How foolish," he told himself. "Nothing on the shore can harm me." And he swam on.

"Stop!" commanded the voice. "I am Tui Vesi, the guardian of Kandavu. How dare you approach my precious island so boldly."

Dakuwaca was rather frightened, but was determined not to show it.

"And I am Dakuwaca, the greatest of all sharks. Come out and fight to defend your island."

"I am a land guardian and so cannot come into the water to fight you," said Tui Vesi. "I shall send one of my servants to fight you instead. But be warned! It is a great and terrible monster, and it would be much better if you left now."

"No-one is braver or stronger than I," said Dakuwaca. "I am not afraid of anything. I will fight your servant." He swam around the mouth of the reef, watching and waiting for his opponent. His body was strong and quick and his teeth were sharp.

Suddenly, a giant arm appeared from the reef and grabbed him. A giant octopus! This wasn't what Dakuwaca was expecting at all!

He thrashed and twisted to rid himself of the arm. His sharp teeth were quite useless because he could not bend his body to bite at the arm. The arm loosened as he twisted and, for a moment, Dakuwaca thought he was free.

But no, two more arms whipped round so that he could no longer move at all. And the arms began to squeeze, tighter and tighter until Dakuwaca could bear it no longer.

"Have mercy," he gasped. "Forgive my terrible presumption, Tui Vesi."

The arms of the octopus loosened slightly, and Tui Vesi's mighty voice boomed out into the waters once more.

"I will release you, Dakuwaca, providing that you promise to guard the people of my island from sharks which might attack them when they go out in their canoes."

"Yes, yes! Of course I will," Dakuwaca agreed.

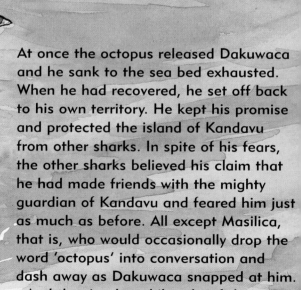

At once the octopus released Dakuwaca and he sank to the sea bed exhausted. When he had recovered, he set off back to his own territory. He kept his promise and protected the island of Kandavu from other sharks. In spite of his fears, the other sharks believed his claim that he had made friends with the mighty guardian of Kandavu and feared him just as much as before. All except Masilica, that is, who would occasionally drop the word 'octopus' into conversation and dash away as Dakuwaca snapped at him.

And that is why, while other fishermen of the Fiji islands fear for their lives because of the sharks, the men of Kandavu ride happily in their canoes.

True or false?

Which of these facts are true and which are false?
If you have read this book carefully, you will know the answers!

1. Almost one-third of the world's surface is covered by oceans.

2. The paws of a polar bear are webbed.

3. Dolphins and whales can stay underwater for several hours.

4. Sound travels through water five times faster than through air.

5. The world's four oceans are the Pacific, the Atlantic, the Aegean and the Mediterranean.

6. It takes 5,000 years for one drop of seawater to travel through all the world's oceans.

7. Tsunamis are caused by underwater volcanic explosions and earthquakes.

8. Plankton is a rich mixture made up of the debris from seaweed.

9. Octopuses have 12 arms and feed mainly on seals.

10. Seaweed is used to help make ice cream.

11. Fish travel in schools until they have learnt how to protect themselves.

12. Sharks must keep moving all the time or they will sink.

ANSWERS: 1.F 2.T 3.F 4.T 5.F 6.T 7.T 8.F 9.F 10.T 11.F 12.T

Glossary

Algae are plants that grow underwater, such as seaweeds.

Bay is part of an ocean or other large body of water that forms a curve in the shoreline. It is bordered on the coastline by headlands or capes.

Continent is a large piece of land or mainland. It is larger than a normal island and usually divided into several countries (except for the continent of Australia).

Current or stream is the movement of a body of water in a particular direction. Ocean currents may be very strong and extend over great distances.

Echo is the repetition of a noise caused by the bouncing back of sound waves from a solid object. Marine mammals such as dolphins use echoes to locate food and to avoid obstacles.

Environment is the set of conditions in the area where an animal lives. The animal's survival depends on how well it can respond to these conditions.

Coral reef is a colourful ridge formation, usually underwater. It is made up of the hard outer casing produced by a colony of millions of tiny animals called polyps.

Extinction is when the last member of a species dies out. This may be due to overhunting by humans, the arrival of a rival animal or plant, or changes in the species' environment.

Gulf is a part of a sea or ocean that loops into the neighbouring coastline. It is narrower at its mouth than a bay.

Land-locked means surrounded by land.

Manganese is a brittle, greyish-white metallic element, often used in making steel.

Marine means connected with the sea. Marine animals are those which live in the sea.

Minerals are chemical compounds found in rocks. Some of them are useful to humans and are mined.

Pearl is a small gem, usually round and white, cream or bluish-grey. It slowly forms as a protective layer around a grain of sand or other object that irritates the soft flesh inside an oyster's shell.

Pesticides are chemicals used to kill pests that feed on crops. Some may be dangerous to other creatures too.

Plankton is a rich mixture of many types of microscopic life. A large variety of sea animals feed on it.

Poles are found at the exact north and south ends of the Earth. Six months of the year are spent in darkness here.

Pollutant is a dirty and poisonous product, such as car fumes, that damages the environment.

Reproduction is when adult creatures produce new, young individuals for the continuation of their species.

Tide is the regular rise and fall of the sea. It is caused by the pull of the Moon and the Sun.

Toxic means poisonous and harmful to life.

Trench is a deep furrow. The Mariana Trench near Guam is the deepest known place in any ocean.

Tsunami is a huge sea wave caused by an underwater earthquake or volcanic eruption.

Work book

Photocopy this sheet and use it to make your own notes.

Work book

Photocopy this sheet and use it to make your own notes.

Loading your INTERFACT disk

INTERFACT is easy to load. But, before you begin, quickly run through the checklist on the opposite page to ensure that your computer is ready to run the program.

Your INTERFACT CD-ROM will run on both PCs with Windows and on Apple Macs. To make sure that your computer meets the system requirements, check the list below.

SYSTEM REQUIREMENTS

PC
- 486DX2/66 Mhz Processor
- Windows 3.1, 3.11, 95, 98 (or later)
- 8 Mb RAM (16 Mb recommended for Windows 95 and 24 Mb recommended for Windows 98)
- VGA colour monitor
- SoundBlaster-compatible soundcard

APPLE MACINTOSH
- 68020 processor
- system 7.0 (or later)
- 16 Mb of RAM

LOADING INSTRUCTIONS

You can run INTERFACT from the disk – you don't need to install it on your hard drive.

PC WITH WINDOWS 95 OR 98

The program should start automatically when you put the disk in the CD drive. If it does not, follow these instructions.

1. Put the disk in the CD drive
2. Open MY COMPUTER
3. Double-click on the CD drive icon
4. Double-click on the icon called OCEANS

PC WITH WINDOWS 3.1 OR 3.11

1. Put the disk in the CD drive
2. Select RUN from the FILE menu in the PROGRAM MANAGER
3. Type D:\OCEANS (Where D is the letter of your CD drive)
4. Press the RETURN key

APPLE MACINTOSH

1. Put the disk in the CD drive
2. Double click on the INTERFACT icon
3. Double click on the icon called OCEANS

CHECKLIST

- Firstly, make sure that your computer and monitor meet the system requirements as set out on page 40.

- Ensure that your computer, monitor and CD-ROM drive are all switched on and working normally.

- It is important that you do not have any other applications, such as wordprocessors, running. Before starting INTERFACT quit all other applications.

- Make sure that any screen savers have been switched off.

- If you are running INTERFACT on a PC with Windows 3.1 or 3.11, make sure that you type in the correct instructions when loading the disk, using a colon (:) not a semi-colon (;) and a back slash (\) not a forward slash (/). Also, do not use any other punctuation or put any spaces between letters.

How to use INTERFACT

INTERFACT is easy to use.
First find out how to load the program
(see page 40) then read these simple
instructions and dive in!

You will find that there are lots of different features to explore.
To select one, operate the controls on the right hand side of the screen. You will see that the main area of the screen changes as you click on to different features.

For example, this is what your screen will look like when you play Something Fishy Is Going On, all about the different parts of a fish's anatomy. Once you've selected a feature, click on the main screen to start playing.

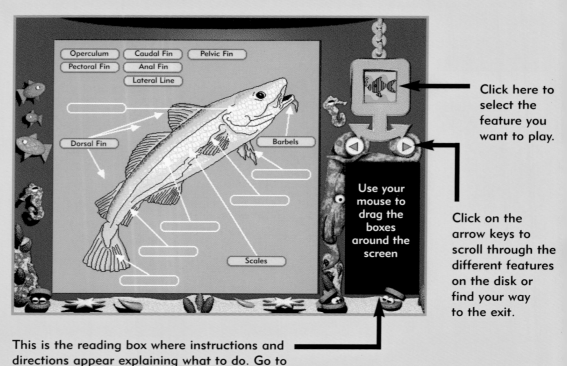

Operculum   Caudal Fin   Pelvic Fin
Pectoral Fin   Anal Fin
Lateral Line

Dorsal Fin

Barbels

Scales

Click here to select the feature you want to play.

Use your mouse to drag the boxes around the screen

Click on the arrow keys to scroll through the different features on the disk or find your way to the exit.

This is the reading box where instructions and directions appear explaining what to do. Go to page 4 to find out what's on the disk.

DISK LINKS

When you read the book, you'll come across Disk Links. These show you where to find activities on the disk that relate to the page you are reading. Use the arrow keys to find the icon on screen that matches the one in the Disk Link.

DISK LINK
Why are sharks' teeth always so sharp? Find out in CREATURE FEATURE.

BOOKMARKS

As you play the features on the disk, you'll bump into Bookmarks. These show you where to look in the book for more information about the topic on screen. Just turn to the page of the book shown in the Bookmark.

23

WORK BOOK

On pages 36–39 you'll find note pages to photocopy and use again and again. Use them to write down your own discoveries as you go through the book and the disk.

HOT DISK TIPS

- After you have chosen the feature you want to play, remember to move the cursor from the icon to the main screen before clicking on the mouse again.

- If you don't know how to use one of the on-screen controls, simply touch it with your cursor. An explanation will pop up in the reading box!

- Keep a close eye on the cursor. When it changes from an arrow ➡ to a hand ☞ click your mouse and something will happen.

- Any words that appear on screen in a different colour and are underlined are 'hot'. This means you can touch them with the cursor for more information.

- Explore the screen! There are secret hot spots and hidden surprises to find.

Troubleshooting

If you have a problem with the INTERFACT disk, you should find the solution here. You can also call the helpline on 01933 443 862. The lines are open from 9am to 5pm, Monday to Friday, and calls are charged at normal rates. But remember to get permission from the person who pays the bill before you use the phone.

QUICK FIXES Run through these general checkpoints before consulting COMMON PROBLEMS (see opposite page).

QUICK FIXES

PC WITH WINDOWS 3.1 OR 3.11

1 Check that you have the minimum specification (see PC specifications on page 40).

2 Make sure you have typed in the correct instructions: a colon (:) not a semi-colon (;) and a back slash (\) not a forward slash (/). Also, do not use punctuation or put any spaces between letters.

3 It is important that you do not have any other programs running. Before you start **INTERFACT**, hold down the Control key and press Escape. If you find that other programs are open, click on them with the mouse, then click the End Task key.

QUICK FIXES

PC WITH WINDOWS 95 or 98

1 Make sure you have typed in the correct instructions: a colon (:) not a semi-colon (;) and a back slash(\) not a forward slash (/). Also, do not use punctuation or put any spaces between letters.

2 It is important that you do not have any other programs running. Before you start **INTERFACT**, look at the task bar. If you find that other programs are open, click on them with the right mouse button and select Close from the pop-up menu.

APPLE MAC

1 Make sure that you have the minimum specification (see specifications on page 40 for Apple Macintosh).

2 It is important that you do not have any other programs running. Before you start **INTERFACT**, click on the application menu in the top right-hand corner. Select each of the open applications and select Quit from the File menu.

COMMON PROBLEMS

Symptom: Cannot load disk.
Problem: There is not enough space available on your hard disk.
Solution: Make more space available by deleting old applications and programs that you are not using.

Symptom: Disk will not run.
Problem: There is not enough memory available.
Solution: *Either* quit other applications and programs (see Quick Fixes) *or* increase your machine's RAM by adjusting the Virtual Memory.

Symptom: Graphics do not load or are poor quality.
Problem: *Either* there is not enough memory available *or* you have the wrong display setting.
Solution: *Either* quit other applications and programs (see Quick Fixes) *or* make sure that your monitor control is set to 256 colours (MAC) or VGA (PC).

Symptom: There is no sound (PCs only).
Problem: Your soundcard is not SoundBlaster compatible.
Solution: Configure sound settings to make them SoundBlaster compatible (see your soundcard manual for more information).

Symptom: Your machine freezes.
Problem: There is not enough memory available.
Solution: *Either* quit other applications and programs (see Quick Fixes) *or* increase your machine's RAM by adjusting the Virtual Memory.

Symptom: Text does not fit neatly into boxes and 'hot' words do not bring up extra information.
Problem: Standard fonts on your computer have been moved or deleted.
Solution: Re-install standard fonts. The PC version requires Arial; the Mac version requires Helvetica. See your computer manual for further information.

Index